Tomorrow's Wish

Tomorrow's Wish

by

Wade Bradford

Characters:

Megan
Juniper
Gary

Mom (Debbie Pomerville)
Dad (David Pomerville)
Gram

The Goochy Brothers: Phil and Bill

Brandi

Justin

Mrs. Dunbar

The Stokeley Sisters

The Set:

The main set consists of the front yard of the
Pomerville house, a friendly place somewhere in
suburban America. A bench, or porch swing,
sits stage right.

Act One:

(*As the lights illuminate the stage, sound effects subtly convey the chirping of birds, the tranquil activities of bees and dragonflies—an array of summertime whisperings.*)

(*Megan Pomerville enters. She looks about 15 or 16 years old. She is tough and energetic, and often restless. She wears rather dark, dreary clothing, especially considering it is summer. She sits down, cross-legged, and opens up a travel magazine. She sighs – absolutely bored.*)

(*Megan's obnoxious younger brother, Gary enters. He carries a recycling can.*)

GARY
Hey ugly.

MEGAN
Good morning, idiot.

GARY
(Sets down recycling can.)
What are you reading?

MEGAN
I'm learning about all the places I'll never visit.

GARY
Are we at Dad's this weekend?

MEGAN
That's next Saturday.
(Back to reading.)
Hey Mom!

(Gary exits. Megan's mother, Debbie
Pomerville enters. She is dressed in a prim
business suit and carries both a purse and a
briefcase.)

                    MEGAN
          (Not realizing that her Mom is outside.)
          Mom!!!

                    MOM
          Now that the neighbors are awake --
          What?

(Gary steps outside to listen.)

                    MEGAN
          I want to go somewhere. Can't we just
          take a two day trip some place? To the
          beach? Or the river?
          The Grand Canyon?

                    GARY
          Or Vegas!

                    MEGAN
          Anywhere.

                    MOM
          We'll do something in August. This
          month, I'm too busy. I have good news,
          though. Grandma is stopping by for a
          surprise visit.

                    GARY
          When?

MOM
Probably now.

MEGAN
(Not thrilled at the idea.)
Is Juniper with her?

GARY
How long is she staying?

MOM
She said she'll only be stopping by for a
few minutes.

MEGAN
It's a five hour drive for her; what's she
doing?

MOM
She didn't give me the details.

GARY
Where is she going?

MOM
You can ask her---

MEGAN
Wait. Did you say Juniper is *staying*
with us? For two weeks?

MOM
That's right.

(This sinks in.)

MEGAN
(Devastated.)
On no.

MOM
You better be nice to her.

MEGAN
But she's such a weirdo!

GARY
And she's very touchy-feely.

MEGAN
And she's embarrassing to be around.

MOM
Megan Pomerville, that is a terrible
thing to say.

MEGAN
I know she's my cousin – but it's the
truth!

MOM
When you were six years old, Juniper
was your best friend in the whole wide
world.

MEGAN
And we used to play house together, and
play with our dolls and have stuffed
animal tea parties, and that was a long
time ago.

MOM
Megan, we've talked about how Juniper
is different.

GARY

It's cuz she's homeschooled. Those
homeschoolers always turn into
goofballs.

MOM

Gary, why would you say something so
rude?

GARY

Well, that's what I heard you say.

MOM

Don't you have chores?

*(Sensing that he's almost in trouble, Gary smiles
and leaves. Megan is darkly amused.)*

MEGAN

So, you called your niece a "goofball."

MOM

I didn't say "goofball." I just said that
some children who happen to be
schooled at home become introverted.
But Juniper is not like that. Listen, I'm
running late as it is. Tell Gram to stop
by the office on her way out of town.
And be on your best behavior with
Juniper. Be nice to her. And do me a
favor; take the Forth of July stuff down,
would you dear?

MEGAN

Why don't you have Gary do it?

GARY
(Entering with second recycle bin.)
I helped put them up. You didn't do
anything, Megan.

MEGAN
Fine.

MOM
And Gary. I want all of those
weeds pulled by this afternoon. No
excuses. *(To Megan.)*
Megan, I'll drop off your job application
in town. *(Megan
doesn't respond.)* You know, now and
then a "thanks Mom" feels pretty good.

MEGAN
(Sarcastic.)
Thanks Mom.

MOM
Be good. *(Leaves.)*

MEGAN
Juniper. Staying with us… I don't know
if I can take it.

GARY
It won't be that bad.

MEGAN
Maybe. Yeah, maybe. It's just that
sometimes she gets excited over the
strangest things.

*(Juniper, a loving, irrepressible young woman,
around Megan's age, runs onto the stage.
Juniper seems different than your average*

teenager – possibly because she appears so whole-heartedly happy. Her shirt is striped and wildly colorful. She wears a jean vest with over a dozen buttons on it.)

(She dashes into the yard, looking around for Megan.)

JUNIPER
Megan! Megan, Megan! It's July the Eighth, Megan. It's Friday again! Can you believe it? Friday, July the Eighth – again! Isn't it wonderful?

MEGAN
(Doesn't care.)
Yeah – uh - I guess it is.

JUNIPER
Megan! Hey little cousin!

(She gives Megan a gigantic hug, lifting her off the ground and squeezing the air out of her.)

MEGAN
It's nice to see you too, Juniper.

GARY
Is grandma here?

JUNIPER
(Reaching out to embrace him.)
Gary!

(A sudden look of fear spreads across Gary's face. Juniper gives him a big hug.)

GARY
Okay, Juniper! Okay. Personal space,
please, personal space!

JUNIPER
Hey guys, check this out, I learned how
to belch-speak the entire periodic table.
(Burping:)
Hydrogen, Helium—

GRAM
Juniper, don't forget your luggage.

*(Megan's Grandma, a spry bespectacled woman
in her late sixties, enters. Juniper and Gary head
out to fetch the luggage.)*

GARY
Hi Gram.

GRAM
Are you helping your cousin with her
luggage, you strong handsome
gentleman, you?

GARY
Yeah. *(Exits with Juniper.)*

MEGAN
Hi Gram.

GRAM
Megan Lee, look at my little bean sprout
of a girl. The school boys must be madly
in love with you.

MEGAN
They've been awfully quiet about it.
Where are you off to this time, Gram?

GRAM
Oh, no where in particular…

MEGAN
Can I go?

GRAM
My, your hair looks –
(Not sure how to compliment her hair.)
-- pretty.

(Gary re-enters. Juniper is with him.)

GARY
Hey, Grandma. Can I have some
money?

GRAM
Give me a hug before you ask about
money. (They hug.) Don't you get an
allowance?

GARY
It's not enough.

GRAM
It never is, kid. Help Juniper take
the bags upstairs.

(Juniper and Gary carry the bags toward the
house.)

MEGAN
So, if I guess this secret location,
will you take me with you?

GRAM
Oh, I'll tell you… when I get back.

MEGAN
It's some boyfriend, isn't it?

GRAM
Goodness, no! Being married to your
grandfather was quite enough for this
old gal.

MEGAN
Okay...but can I ask... Why exactly are
you leaving Juniper with us?

GRAM
You don't want to spend time with your
cousin?

MEGAN
Sure I do.

GRAM
She only sees you twice a year, yet she
talks about you and Gary almost every
day.

MEGAN
Really?

GRAM
Back home she's got only me, the dogs,
the five cats and the two hamsters, and
the farm critters. Living in the middle of
the boondocks, she doesn't have any
friends her age. That's why this visit
means so much to her.

MEGAN
Does she still collect those Japanese
dolls?

GRAM

She's moved on to antique buttons. Are
you still friends with Brandi?

MEGAN

Just barely. She's acting like a b—

GRAM

Well! I'm sure Juniper would love to
meet some of your girlfriends – the nice
ones, at least. Remember, even though
she's your age, Juniper is very... what's
the word—

MEGAN

Strange?

GRAM

No. Megan. Sensitive. It's my fault,
I'm sure. Words are very important to
her. So be mindful of her feelings. And
choose your words carefully.
This is the first visit she's had without
me hovering over her, and I'm relying
on you to be a good influence.

MEGAN

Okay. I promise.

GRAM

Now give Gram a squeeze; it's time to
go.

*(Juniper and Gary have returned. Juniper
attaches herself to Gram's arm.)*

JUNIPER

Do you have to go now?

GRAM
Yes, June-bug.

JUNIPER
Are you sure?

GRAM
Yes.

JUNIPER
Absolutely positive? *(Gram nods.)* Then
Farewell! Parting is such sweet sorrow
that I could say goodnight until
tomorrow!

GRAM
Bye, bye, sweet-ones. *(To Juniper.)*
And remember everything I told you.

MEGAN and GARY
Bye.

JUNIPER
Bye bye! *(She waves her hand very fast,
flapping it back and forth comically.)*

(Gram exits. Juniper continues to wave.)

JUNIPER
See you grandma!

*(Juniper turns back to the others, with a sigh of
contentment. Her arm is still frantically waving
back and forth. She looks at it in mock
surprise.)*

JUNIPER
I can't stop!

(She grabs her hand and laughs.)

JUNIPER
No, I'm fine – it was just a joke!
(She laughs – highly amused with herself. Her laughter fades when she sees no one is amused.)

MEGAN
So…

JUNIPER
So… The place looks nice. Where's the tree house?

GARY
It got infested with termites and we tore it down. I'm hungry. Are you hungry?

JUNIPER
I'm always hungry.

GARY
Do you like pie?

JUNIPER
The food or the mathematical constant?

GARY
Huh?

JUNIPER
Pi, you know: 3.1415926535--

GARY
It's apple pie.

JUNIPER
Oh, that's good too.

(Gary exits.)

JUNIPER
So, without the tree house, what do you
do for fun around here?

MEGAN
Oh, whatever we want to do.

JUNIPER
Awesome. *(She takes out five books
from her back pack. She gets ready to
read.)* Let's get this party started. *(She
becomes instantly engrossed in a book.)*

MEGAN
So, is this what you do all day at
Gram's?

JUNIPER
This? Boy, that would be nice! No, I
can't always sit around and read. Gotta
feed the sheep, collect the eggs from the
hen house, tend to the goats, feed the
goldfish. Hey, maybe this summer you
could work on the ranch.

MEGAN
I'm allergic to every animal you named.

JUNIPER
Even the goldfish?

MEGAN
Especially the goldfish.

(Gary enters with two servings of pie. He hands one to Juniper.)

MEGAN
Hey idiot, where's mine?

GARY
Let me think, ugly. It's in the fridge waiting for you to cut it yourself.

JUNIPER
Ow. Why would you say that to each other?

GARY
She likes it.

JUNIPER
Are you allergic to goldfish too?

GARY
What?

JUNIPER
I just think it's so sad about Megan.

MEGAN
Well what about you? Do you have any *two legged* friends?

JUNIPER
The ducks.

MEGAN
I mean like humans.

JUNIPER
Well, Grammy's my friend.

MEGAN
Family doesn't count.

JUNIPER
Why not?

MEGAN
Because you're stuck with family. You choose your friends.

JUNIPER
Oh. I never thought of that.

MEGAN
It must be so lonely for you. I don't know how you can stand it.

JUNIPER
But I love my home—

(Gary finishes his pie and exits, taking his plate.)

MEGAN
But you don't even live next to a school. And the nearest town is what?

JUNIPER
52.6 miles away.

MEGAN
Don't you ever wish—

JUNIPER
No. I never do.

MEGAN
Well, this summer, we'll have to have
you find your own set of friends; not my
friends, but human friends. *(Shuts
Juniper's book.)* Besides
Charles Dickens.

JUNIPER
But you're my friend.

MEGAN
We're cousins. I'm talking about non-
relative type people. You need your
own circle.

JUNIPER
Circles are beautiful.

MEGAN
And you might want to stop saying
things.

JUNIPER
Do you have a lot of friends?

MEGAN
Yeah. Some of them are jerks, though.

JUNIPER
What about boys?

MEGAN
You mean guys? Like to go out with?

JUNIPER
Oh, have you been out on dates?

MEGAN
Not very often.

JUNIPER
"Not often" is way more often than me.
Do you have a boyfriend?

MEGAN
Not anymore.

JUNIPER
Oh, Meg – Is your heart broken?

MEGAN
No! It was just – we barely even dated.
It was a half-date, really, and now we're
just friends.

JUNIPER
Friends are a wonderful thing.

MEGAN
Not really. Not when it's a guy you like
and you want to be more than friends.
Then friendship sucks.

JUNIPER
What's his name?

MEGAN
Justin. But it's not a big deal. He and
Brandi are together now. They have
been for a while.

JUNIPER
I've never met Brandi. Is she your best
friend?

MEGAN
Well, she—

JUNIPER
Maybe I can meet her. Have you ever
read "The Three Musketeers"? Maybe
we could all—

MEGAN
I don't think so.

JUNIPER
(A bit hurt by this.)
Why?

MEGAN
You're a little too bubbly for my circle.

(Gary comes back in.)

JUNIPER
But bubbles *are* circular, or spherical at
least. Hey—do you like my button
collection? *(Shows her buttons on
jacket.)* I picked this one out for your
dad, because he likes beer. Hey, where
is Uncle David?

GARY
Dad doesn't live with us right now.

MEGAN
You mean "anymore."

GARY
They're just on a break.

MEGAN
Forever.

JUNIPER

Oh no. Grammy said something about
a trial separation, but I thought it was
jury duty.

MEGAN

Trial separation is what parents call it
before they sign the divorce papers.

GARY

Shut up, Megan!

MEGAN

You shut up!

GARY

No you.

MEGAN

Why don't you stop talking to us and
pull all the weeds like you're supposed
to.

JUNIPER

Guys, please don't fight. Gary, do you
need any help with the yard?

GARY

No, that's okay.

MEGAN

Then hurry up and do it.

GARY

Don't tell me when to do my chores.

MEGAN

You're a lazy piece of snot.

GARY
You're a handful of farts.

JUNIPER
I don't remember you guys talking this
way around Christmas time.

(Sound Cue: An old truck sputters to a stop.)

*(Megan and Gary hear this and smiles come to
their faces.)*

GARY
Dad!

*(In walks their father, Dave Pomerville. He is a
mechanic, and dresses like one: greasy jumpsuit,
baseball hat, wrench in his shirt pocket, hands
black with oil.)*

DAD
Hey kids.

(Juniper runs up to hug him.)

JUNIPER
Uncle David!

DAD
Well hello there, Juniper! Careful, now.
You'll wrinkle my business suit.

MEGAN
Drove the pick-up?

DAD
Could you hear it? Purrs like a kitten.

GARY

And barks like a dog.

DAD

Speaking of which, is your mom home?

MEGAN

Still at work.

GARY

Hey Dad! Got anything excited planned
for next weekend?

DAD

Ohhh… maybe.

MEGAN

That means no.

DAD

Well, as much as I'd love to stay and
chat with Princess Cheerful, I've got to
get back to work. Keep up the good
fight with those weeds, Gary.

GARY

I'll try. Bye Dad.

MEGAN

Bye.

DAD

See you, kids. Keep them out of
trouble, Juniper. *(He exits.)*

*(She laughs. Gary kneels to the ground and
heaves a heavy sigh.)*

GARY
This will take forever. Megan gets to
take down a few flags. I have to take
care of a yard that's as big as an
ocean. Hey, that gives me an idea.

(He jumps to his feet and runs into the house.)

JUNIPER
Why did your Dad call you Princess
Cheerful?

MEGAN
He was being sarcastic.

JUNIPER
So you aren't a Princess?

MEGAN
No.

JUNIPER
Darn. I've always wanted to be related
to royalty.

*(Gary comes back out with his Fishing Pole. A
small rubber fish is attached to the line.)*

MEGAN
What about your chores?

GARY
I'm on a break.

JUNIPER
What are you doing?

GARY
Yard fishing.

(He casts out the rubber fish. Ideally the fish will be cast off either center stage, right down the aisle—or, perhaps more practical cast off stage left.)

GARY (Cont'd.)
This is how I practice, in case I ever fish for real. But all I ever do is yard fish. Remember, Megan, when
Dad would take us out to the lake? 'Member that catfish I caught?

JUNIPER
How big was it?

GARY
(Stretches out his arms.)
At least this big.

MEGAN
Half that size, Gary.

GARY
(Reeling in and casting out again.)
Dad says he'll take me deep sea fishing one day. When business at the shop slows down. So that'll be about never. But just think. *(Reels, casts.)* Casting out into the open water. Snagging a sea bass, or a hundred pound halibut, or the mother of all sports-fisherman trophies—a twenty foot shark. *(Sigh.)* I'm tired of dinking around in the yard with these dumb old toys. I wish I was fishing for real. Right now.

JUNIPER
Okey-doke.

(All of a sudden, there is a sharp tug on Gary's line. It stuns everyone—especially Gary. Then, after the tug, the line zips away, as if a mighty fish was swimming away with the hook.)

MEGAN
What did you do?!!

GARY
Maybe I caught a squirrel!

(Gary starts reeling. Suddenly, he is yanked to the ground. He struggles to his knees, pulling back on the pole with all of his might.)

MEGAN
Maybe you're hooked onto a truck! Just let it go!

GARY
Are you kidding?! I'm not losing my pole. I'm reeling this sucker in!

(SOUND FX: Bushes rustling. The three gaze off stage, awe-struck.)

JUNIPER
I see something moving in the bushes!

MEGAN
I think I see a... a...

GARY
A shark fin!

(SOUND FX: Huge splash. Ocean noise. For comic effect – play "Jaws" music.)

(Note: Depending upon staging ability, there way even be a shark fin visible in the background or foreground – but this idea is completely optional.)

MEGAN
It's a fish!

JUNIPER
It's a big fish!

GARY
It's a shark!

MEGAN
There's a shark in our rhododendron!

(SOUND FX: SPLASH.)

(Gary is yanked back to the ground. Megan grabs onto him, and now – if possible— they are both being pulled away. Juniper grabs Megan's arm or leg.)

GARY
I can't hold on!

MEGAN
Just let it go!

(Gary tries one more time to pull the beast in, but he loses his grip and the fishing pole flies from his hands, and is whisked off stage.)

(SOUND FX: There is a final splash sound effect. And an echoing gurgle indicating that the unseen creature has gone away.)

(Gary, Megan, and Juniper slowly stand up. They are exhausted, not knowing exactly what has happened.)

GARY
Did you see it? Did you see that thing?

JUNIPER
Wow.

GARY
It must have jumped ten feet in the air and splashed down... But how could it... I mean... It was like it splashed into the grass... Like the lawn had turned into water, just for a second...

(Megan has been dialing a cell phone.)

MEGAN
(On phone.)
Hello. Animal control? I want to report a stray fish. (Pause.) Yes. (Pause.) About two hundred pounds.
(Pause.) Yeah, a loose fish. Come on down if you don't believe me. He's probably flopping around on Maple Street by now.

(Mom enters the scene. She carries a bag of groceries.)

MOM
Who are you talking to?

MEGAN
(Puts phone away.)
Oh, no one. Salesperson.

GARY
Mom. You'll never believe it. We saw
a...

(Megan quickly covers Gary's mouth.)

MEGAN
We didn't see anything.

JUNIPER
We saw a giant shark on Gary's hook,
and it had huge fins, big mean eyes, and
teeth like a demon.

*(During Juniper's explanation, Mom steps
towards the house; then she pauses, and finds
Juniper's description very curious.)*

MEGAN
They were just playing a game. You
know, looking at shapes in the clouds.

(Mom stares up at the sky. She tilts her head.)

MOM
Oh yeah. I can see it.

(She goes inside.)

GARY
Why didn't you tell her the truth?

MEGAN
Because she'll think we're crazy!

GARY
But it was real.

JUNIPER
It looked real.

MEGAN
It couldn't have been real.

MOM
(From off stage.)
Juniper! Megan! Come help me fix
dinner.

MEGAN
Okay.

*(Juniper happily runs into the house. Megan,
less excited, follows. She picks up her drink,
suspicious.)*

MEGAN (Cont'd.)
Mom… what was in the lemonade?

*(Megan exits. Gary brushes himself off. He
scans the distance in search of marine life, and
now skips upstairs to enter the house. But Mom
is there to halt him.)*

MOM
And did we finish our chores today?

GARY
Uh…

MOM

I see we didn't weed the yard. There's a
lot of daylight left. You get to it, mister.

GARY

(Scared of the shark's return.)
Mom... can I do it tomorrow?

MOM

No. You'll do it now, and you'll get it
done before dinner. And don't look at
me with those angry eyes.

*(She exits. Gary slowly, timidly picks up a rake
and heads out into the yard.)*

GARY

It's not anger. It's fear.

*(He picks up the rake, holding it as if to guard
himself. He looks around, scared. Juniper
pokes her head out the window to watch him,
very amused.)*

GARY

Here fishy, fishy, fishy. Nice "yard
fishy." Hmm. I guess he's gone.

(Juniper pokes her head into the scene and yells
"Boo!" Gary screams!)

LIGHTS DOWN.

SCENE TWO: The next day.

(It's morning. Mom steps into the yard. She wears jogging attire. She stretches for a moment and then starts to jog. Gary leaps out the front door.)

GARY
Don't go on the grass!!!

(This startles his mother. She halts suddenly, almost trips.)

MOM
Why not?!

GARY
(Making something up.)
Because... I cleaned up the yard... and I just want to keep it nice.

MOM
Oh. *(A bit patronizingly.)* Okay. I'll be back in a few.

(She jogs off stage. Megan steps onto the porch.)

MEGAN
Did you tell her anything?

GARY
Of course not.

MEGAN
Good. Because I think I've figured everything out. We experienced a massive hallucination.

GARY
We did not.

MEGAN
Just listen—Each of us were bored out
of our minds.

*(Juniper steps out. She's carrying four boxes of
cereal and a bowl.)*

JUNIPER
Who wants breakfast?

GARY
Morning Juniper.

*(She sits down and proceeds to pour cereal into
the large bowl—two boxes at a time.)*

MEGAN
We were sitting outside in the hot sun.
It's like being out in the desert and
seeing a mirage.

GARY
It wasn't a mirage. I've figured out
what really happened.

JUNIPER
Is there milk in the fridge?

MEGAN
Yes.

*(Juniper goes back inside, leaving behind her
mountain of cereal.)*

GARY

I was out there pulling weeds. After
working hard for a very long time, I
took a little break and sat right there
with my old fishing pole. I then made a
wish. You remember?

MEGAN
(Doubtful.)
Yes.

GARY

And it came true. Don't you get it? My
fishing pole is magic. It grants wishes!

MEGAN
You're nuts.

(Juniper re-enters with milk.)

JUNIPER
Who's nuts?

MEGAN
Your cousin Gary.

JUNIPER
Oh. I already know that.

(Dad enters carrying a tool kit.)

DAD
Good morning trouble makers.

GARY
Dad, what are you doing here?

DAD
I thought you might be tired of all this heat.

MEGAN
Let me guess: Goochy's Junkyard.

DAD
It almost works too. Bring it on in, fellas.

(Two big strong men in dirty work clothes lumber onto the stage carrying a rusty, clanky old air conditioning system. Actually, it's more of a "swamp cooler" than a system. These two gentlemen are the seemingly lunk-headed Goochy Brothers: Phil and Bill.)

MEGAN
Hi Phil. Hi Bill.

PHIL
Hey.

BILL
Hey.

DAD
Just set it down in the den.

GARY
It's a sewing room now.

DAD
Oh yeah.

(Phil and Bill trudge toward the house.)

DAD
Make sure you don't break the—

(CRASH Sound Effect. Something has been broken. Megan and Juniper run to see.)

DAD
Never mind. (To Gary.) Hey sport, did you lose something recently?

GARY
What?

DAD
I found this. (Opens tool box.) It's broken but I can fix it.

(He removes a broken fishing pole.)

GARY
All right! Thanks Dad!

DAD
I found it half way up Maple Street. It shouldn't be too difficult to repair.

GARY
No, no, it's good. Now watch this, Dad. You'll never believe what this can do.
(He raises the pole aloft in the air.)
I wish I had a million dollars!

(Dad stares. Gary looks around. Nothing.)

GARY
I said: I wish for a million dollars.

DAD
Gary?

GARY

Darn it!

(Gary stomps off, annoyed. He exits just as Megan and Juniper enter.)

MEGAN

Phil and Bill are trying to repair the coffee table, but they're mostly just scratching up the hardwood floor.

DAD

Aw man. Guys! Just worry about the air conditioner. How long has your mother been jogging?

MEGAN

About five minutes.

DAD

Oh no. She'll be back soon.

(After a brief moment, Mom slumps in, huffing and puffing. She is apparently the world's wimpiest jogger. She pants and moans. Then, she sees Dad. She straightens herself up, and presses a button on her watch. It beeps.)

MOM
(Pretending to be satisfied.)
Two hours and ten minutes. Good morning, David. You do realize they're *yours next* weekend.

DAD

They're mine all the time.

MOM
Okay, they're ours. And you know
that's not what I mean. Why are you
here?

DAD
Well, I brought over a surprise.

(There's another loud crash inside.)

MOM
What kind of a surprise? The kind
That you bring over because you
Have bad news.

DAD
Not exactly. Well. See, next weekend, I
can't take the kids.

MEGAN
You jerk.

MOM
Megan!

DAD
It's a long story. Work related.

MOM
Surprise, surprise.

DAD
And speaking of surprises--
The weekend after next, I
have baseball tickets. Five tickets to be
exact.

MEGAN
There's no baseball team around here.

DAD

Sixty miles out of town. A little road
trip and we'll all be able to watch the
Gorman Tigers.

JUNIPER

That's Grandpa's old team!

MOM

(Trying not to smile, but smiling.)
He was just the assistant coach.

JUNIPER

I bet he sits up on a cloud and watches
every game.

MOM

(Touches Juniper's shoulder.)
I do too, sweetie.

DAD

So whatdaya say? We could make the
weekend of it.

MOM

Together? I don't know... I'd have to
check my calendar... And really, if the
two of us were stuck together in a car
for more than— *(Looks toward house.)*
What did you do to my house?!

DAD

Surprise! You got a new air
conditioner!

MOM

Oh no, is that Phil and Bill?

(Carrying odds and ends, Phil and Bill walk on stage.)

PHIL

Hey.

BILL

Hey.

MOM

My floor!

(She moves towards the house, fuming. Dad follows, trying to calm down.)

DAD

Now, now, it's not so bad.

(Mom and Dad exit. More noise—ad lib shouting and fighting—from inside. Gary enters.)

GARY

Another fight?

MEGAN

Uh-huh.

GARY

Well, we haven't had one of those in a while. I forgot how loud they were.

JUNIPER

It makes me so sad to hear it. They're so angry. Gary, turn on the radio so we can listen to something happy.

*(Gary turns on the portable radio. Peppy
Ranchero music plays.)*

GARY
Let me see.

*(The argument inside the house (a muffle of
shouts and angry words) grows louder too. Phil
and Bill enter from the back of the house; they
carry the old swamp cooler. Megan paces back
and forth, frustrated by the noise and hostility
from inside the house.)*

PHIL
We're gonna have to crack this thing
open.

BILL
Yep.

(Phil starts to hammer the swamp cooler.)

MEGAN
(Covering her ears.)
Ugh! I can't take it. I wish everyone
would just shut up for a minute!

JUNIPER
Okey-doke.

*(All of a sudden, everything is silent on stage.
No more yelling from inside the house. No more
noise from the radio. Even the hammer is silent,
although Phil still appears to slam it against the
cooler.)*

*(Megan and Gary are stunned and bewildered.
Juniper seems a bit pleased. She sits with a
sketch pad and doodles.)*

(Phil and Bill are very confused. Phil examines the hammer.)

(Megan panics, tries to yell, touches her throat; she is scared and confused.)

(Gary can't speak either, and then goes through the same panic as his sister.)

(She mouths: CAN YOU HEAR ME?)

(He shakes his head: NO! Megan and Gary then frantically gesture to Juniper, who just shrugs and shakes her head with a smile.)

(Suddenly, the music begins again.)

MEGAN
What's happen--- I can talk again!

GARY
And hear. *(Shuts off radio.)*

PHIL *(To Bill)*
Something's wrong with my hammer.

(He hammers the swamp cooler loudly.)

PHIL
That's better.

GARY
What just happened?

(Mom and Dad enter—rather confused.)

MOM
--for a minute I thought I had gone deaf.

DAD
Maybe we were yelling so loud we
lost our voices.

MOM
Look, David, I appreciate what you
were trying to do...But you come over
here, unexpectedly, it just gets—

DAD
I know...

MOM
Let's talk later, okay?

DAD
Phil. Bill. Let's head back to the shop.
See you, kids.

MEGAN
Bye, Dad.

JUNIPER
Bye, Uncle David!

(Dad, Phil and Bill exit.)

MOM
(Looking to kids, rubbing her ears.)
Did anything strange—

MEGAN
No.

MOM
Hmm... Oh well. Will you kids help me
clean up my once beautiful home?

GARY
More chores. Terrific.

MEGAN
(Lingering behind.)
We'll be right there…

*(Gary and Mom go inside the house. Megan sits
on the porch step next to Juniper.)*

MEGAN
(Careful, quiet and serious.)
Juniper. Do you know what's going on?

(She nods her head.)

MEGAN
Will you tell me?

JUNIPER
What do you want to know?

MEGAN
How did all of the sound go away? I
mean, I wished for everyone to shut
up—and then everything did.

JUNIPER
Grammy says its best to not tell
anybody. But sometimes I think it
would feel good to let go of the words,
and just blurt the secret out.

MEGAN
The secret?

JUNIPER
Uh-huh.

MEGAN
Juniper… Can you… can you make
wishes come true?

*(Juniper stares at her for a long moment. She
looks around, and then she nods.)*

MEGAN
(Calm at first then excited.)
Oh. I knew it. *(Pause.)* I KNEW IT!
This is fantastic! I can't believe it! We
can do anything, Juniper! I… I…
I WISH I COULD FLY!

*(Megan leaps into the air and tumbles to the
ground. Juniper runs to her side.)*

JUNIPER
Megan! Are you okay?

MEGAN
It didn't work. But I thought you said…

JUNIPER
There are rules, Megan. And you have
to pay attention to the rules.

MEGAN
Wait, wait. Is this like a hypnosis trick.
You can fool people into seeing things
or hearing things.

JUNIPER
Fool people?

MEGAN
You know, mess with their brains.

JUNIPER
Oh, I wouldn't want to do something
like that. It sounds painful.

MEGAN
Okay, then explain it to me. How do
you make these things happen?

JUNIPER
I don't know how I do it. But Grandma
says it started happening when I when I
was six. That's sort of one of the
reasons, I don't see you as much as I
did... Things changed afterwards.

MEGAN
What kinds of wishes have you made?

JUNIPER
(Laughs, then:)
Oh, I don't make the wishes, Megan.
Other people do. And I'm a good
listener. But Grammy says I shouldn't
listen to everybody -- if I don't want to.
But it's hard to say no sometimes.
So we keep to ourselves pretty much.

MEGAN
Is that why you and Gram live so far
away? Hey, so if Grandma knows about
this -- If she can make wishes
anytime she wants, why do I always get
a lousy sweater for Christmas?

JUNIPER
Gram doesn't usually wish for anything.
Except by accident. Not on purpose.
Just accidental, like, "I wish that faucet
would stop leakin'" Or, "I wish those

JUNIPER (Cont'd.)
dogs would quit their barkin'." But she
hasn't made an mistake like that in a
long time.

MEGAN
So, the dogs stopped barking forever?

JUNIPER
No, just a day. The wish only goes for a
day. When the sun goes down, it stops
working. When the sun comes back up,
you can make another.

MEGAN
So if I wish for a hundred thousand
dollars into my bank account?

JUNIPER
It's there for a while and then: Poof.
Bye-bye before the next day. At least
that's what Grandma says.

MEGAN
Temporary wishes? Hmm. (Pause.)
But Juniper... If what you're saying is
true, why couldn't I fly?

JUNIPER
Only one wish a day. You have to wait
till morning. But would you really want
to fly? What if you got hit by an
airplane?

MEGAN
You're right. It was silly. I'll have to
think of something worth while. You
don't mind, do you? You know, if I
make a wish.

JUNIPER
You'd only wish for good things, right?

MEGAN
Sure, of course. But I still don't know
that I believe all this.

JUNIPER
Well, tomorrow you'll see. Now let's
see if where do you keep your art
supplies? I feel like painting up a storm
(Grabs her by the hand, runs off.)

*(Gary enters. He holds his broken fishing pole.
He's been listening to this whole conversation.)*

GARY
Interesting… *(Smiles deviously.)*

(He tosses the fishing pole to the ground.)

LIGHTS OUT.

END OF ACT ONE.

ACT TWO / SCENE ONE:

(The next day. Megan steps into the yard, yawning and stretching.)

MEGAN
I didn't mean to sleep so late. Juniper.
(Looks around.) Juniper?

(Juniper skips into the scene, fastening a new button onto her jacket.)

JUNIPER
Look Megan, I got a new button.

MEGAN
(Takes out a piece of folded paper.)
Okay, okay. Around three a.m. I made this list. I wrote out all of my wishes and then arranged them in order of importance.

JUNIPER
Gary gave it to me as a present.

MEGAN
But before we start I've got a whole bunch of questions for you.

JUNIPER
Isn't it pretty, Megan?

MEGAN
First of all, if I wish for something, and I don't like it—

JUNIPER
Megan, look at my button...

MEGAN

I see your stupid button, okay?! Now
will you listen to me?

*(This hurts Juniper. She looks down at the
ground. Then she sits, saddened.)*

MEGAN
(Sits beside her. Apologetic.)
Look.... I just want to see if it
really works. And if it does, I promise,
you and I will have the best summer
ever. Now, let's test it out. *(Stands.
Summons up a commanding voice.)*
Juniper, I wish I had my driver's license.
(Closes eyes and holds out her hand.)

*(Nothing happens. Juniper simply looks at her.
Megan opens her eyes.)*

MEGAN
It didn't work?

JUNIPER
You can't have your wish today.

MEGAN
But... I... you said *(A look of
realization.)* So you tricked me. And I
can't believe I fell for it. Wishes! Ha! I
thought they were real! I thought your
story was real, Juniper! Don't worry,
I'm not mad at you. In fact, I'm
impressed. You really had me fooled.
*(Sits down and laughs a bit,
then lets out a sigh to relieve the stress.)*
Yep. You got me.

JUNIPER

Megan, you can't have your wish today
because Gary already used it.

(Megan becomes rigid. Her eyes widen.)

MEGAN

He... *what?!*

JUNIPER

Sorry.

MEGAN

Gary!!!

(She storms toward the house.)

MEGAN

Gary! Are you in your room? Get out
here this instant.

GARY *(From off stage.)*
(Muffled, fearful voice.)

I can't.

(Megan storms back out onto the porch.)

MEGAN

That annoying little—ugh! He stole it
from me. What could that brainless little
twit possibly wish for? Gary?!

*(She storms off stage. Then, she shrieks. She
storms back.)*

MEGAN

Oh my gosh... His bedroom is
completely filled with... with...

(Gary crawls onto the stage. He has gummy bears in his hair, and gummy bears clenched in both fists.)

GARY

Gummy bears! I almost drowned in them!

(Gary composes himself, then coughs. A few gummy bears plop out of his mouth.)

MEGAN

What did you do?

GARY

I talked to Juniper and wished for a million gummy bears.

MEGAN

Why did you do that?

GARY

I was gonna wish for money, but I was hungry. I figure I can eat some of them and sell the rest.

MEGAN
(Annoyed.)

So, you know about our little secret. Did you also know that you wasted a wish? And that it was supposed to be mine?

GARY

Boo hoo. You were asleep. And if you had it your way, you never would have told me about her magical powers.

MEGAN
Because you'd do something stupid.
And you did!

JUNIPER
Don't be mad, Megan. It's my fault. I
should have waited for you.

MEGAN
(To Gary.)
I still say you're an idiot. You don't
realize what you're dealing with.
Juniper is a walking talking
miracle. For all we know she's a gift
sent directly from heaven. What she
can do is... is... pure unexplainable
magic. Impossible magic.
Something so much bigger than
ourselves; it's something cosmic,
something that might be divine.

GARY
You wished for a driver's license, didn't
you?

MEGAN
Yes! I wished for a driver's license! So
what? *(Paces around the porch.)* Enjoy
your gummy bears. Have fun.
Tomorrow, I get to have
a wish, Gary, otherwise I am going to
strangle you!

(Megan exits.)

JUNIPER
I think she's mad.

GARY
I guess it wasn't the smartest wish.

JUNIPER
But aren't you happy, Gary?

GARY
I guess. But Mom's gonna freak out
if she goes into my bedroom.

JUNIPER
You wanna hang out with me?

GARY
Nah... I got too much to do.
I've got to package up some gummy
bears and start selling them. Wish me
luck!

JUNIPER
Good luck.

(Gary exits. Juniper is alone. Lights fade.)

SCENE TWO:
*(Lights return. Megan and Juniper are sitting
on the porch swing. Gary can be heard inside
his bedroom counting pennies. The mom jogs
once or twice across the yard.)*

GARY
Six hundred forty two... Six
hundred forty three...

MEGAN
He's been counting bags of gummy
bears all day.

JUNIPER
Your brother is very industrious.
I don't think he knows that the wish is
temporary.

MEGAN
Let's not tell him.

JUNIPER
It's a pretty sunset; don't you think?
It would be lovely to paint. Megan, let's
do portraits tomorrow. Will you help
me?

MEGAN
Sure.

JUNIPER
It's beautiful sunset though. Guess I'll
just have to capture it with a mental
photograph. "Click." *(She pretends to
take a picture.)*

MEGAN
So... what happens to the gummy bears
at sundown?

JUNIPER
They'll just go bye-bye...

MEGAN
I wonder how he'll take it.

*(Lights fade down slowly, as Gary continues to
count. In the darkness:)*

GARY (Off stage.)
Six hundred fifty eight—*("Magic"
Sound FX)*

59

GARY (Off stage.)
Huh? *They're gone!* NOOOOOO!!!!!!

SCENE THREE:
(The Next Day. Megan enters; she is going over a list of different wishes. Gary sits on the steps, his head in his hands. Juniper is setting up her paints.)

JUNIPER
Good morning. You're just in time to pose for me.

MEGAN
Oh, not right now, I'm too excited.
Hey idiot, did you steal my wish?

GARY
No ugly. I didn't steal it. Who cares about magical wishes if they're just going to fade away?

MEGAN
They last for a whole day – think of all the possibilities; you know, besides a stupid room full of candy.

GARY
Why is everything crossed off your list?

MEGAN
I can't decide what to wish for first.
And I don't want to screw things up like that Monkey Paw.

JUNIPER
Monkey paw?

GARY
Oh, it's this awesome story about this
guy who wishes to see his dead son
again, and this zombie comes knocking
on his door.

JUNIPER
Oh that's gross.

GARY
You wouldn't make something like that
happen, would you?

JUNIPER
Oh, no, well, I don't really control it—

MEGAN
Hey, wait… How do you do it, Juniper?

GARY
Yeah, are you part genie or something?

JUNIPER
No. I don't know how it works. I used
to do it a lot, you know, make stuff
happen, mostly by accident, or
whenever Mama would ask me.
That's when I lived with her. But since
I've been at Gram's it hasn't come up
in a while.

GARY
Gram doesn't make wishes? What, is
she crazy?

MEGAN
That's what I said!

JUNIPER
While you're making your wish list,
can you pose for my painting?

MEGAN
I'm too nervous. I can't think
straight. There's too many things I want
to do.

JUNIPER
You just need to stand right here.

MEGAN
Uh, Gary will help you.

GARY
Help what?

MEGAN
With her painting.

GARY
Ugh! I just painted the fence two weeks
ago.

MEGAN
No, idiot, she's painting a picture.

JUNIPER
I need someone to pose for me.

GARY
Oh, I can do that.
(Strikes a heroic pose.)

JUNIPER
(Sets up her painting material.)
Perfect!

MEGAN
Good. Now, I'm brainstorming, so
don't you dare steal my wish.

(Megan exits.)

GARY
(Sticks out tongue.)
Pfffftt!

JUNIPER
Hold still.

GARY
(Standing still.)
How long will this take?

JUNIPER
They say that before completing his
Mona Lisa, Leonardo Da Vinci studied
his subject for six months

GARY
Oh great.

JUNIPER
Here, let's make your pose a little more
compelling. *(She puts some Roman garb
on him, hands him a sword and a bowl
of fruit.)* Now hold still – I need a
smaller brush.

*(Juniper dashes off. Gary sighs. Megan enters.
She looks at him.)*

MEGAN
(Angry.)
You used another wish, didn't you?!

GARY
Yes, I am now the Emperor of Planet
Earth. You think I'd wish to look like
this?!

(Brandi enters. She is Megan's friend and rival.)

BRANDI
Hi guys. Wow Gary. I like the new
look.

MEGAN
Hi Brandi.

BRANDI
Is your cousin still in town?

MEGAN
Yeah.

BRANDI
So she's really, uh… different, isn't
she?

MEGAN
You could say that.
(Changing the subject.)
You wanna watch a movie or something
tonight?

BRANDI
Actually, Justin is taking me out to
dinner. Sixth month anniversary. But I
can't find anything to wear.

GARY
You can borrow my toga.

BRANDI
Ha. Meg, can you help me out?

MEGAN
Sure, you can wear whatever.

BRANDI
Do you still have the green dress?

MEGAN
Uh, yeah, but I don't know if you'd
want to wear that one…

BRANDI
Why not? I love it.

(Juniper enters.)

MEGAN
That's the outfit I wore… you know,
when me and Justin—

BRANDI
Oh. On your one date together.

GARY
Megan, you told me it was only half a
date.

MEGAN
Shut up.

BRANDI
And they didn't even like each other.
(To Juniper.) I made sure I got Megan's
okay before I made my move. But
I don't need the dress, if it makes
you feel uncomfortable.

MEGAN

No, not if you don't care. Then I don't
mind. It's waiting for you in my closet.

BRANDI

Really? You're so cool.
(To Juniper.)
Your Megan's cousin? Hi, I'm Brandi.
Cool art stuff.

JUNIPER

Hi.

MEGAN

(To Brandi.)
Come on.

*(Megan and Brandi exit towards the house.
Juniper returns to painting.)*

GARY

Can't you just take a picture?

JUNIPER

It's not the same.

GARY

This is boring.

JUNIPER

Art is never boring. It's delightfully
tedious.

(Justin enters.)

JUSTIN

Hey, what's going on?

GARY
Public humiliation.

JUNIPER
Hello.

JUSTIN
Hey. Who's your friend, Gary?

GARY
This is Juniper. My cousin.

JUSTIN
What's up.

JUNIPER
Are you Justin?

JUSTIN
Yep.

JUNIPER
Nice.

JUSTIN
Is Brandi here?

JUNIPER
She's upstairs. She'll be down soon.
(To Gary.)
Okay, Gary, you can take a break.

GARY
Thank you. *(Stomps off.)*

JUNIPER
Remember your pose!

JUSTIN
So, uh, what's she doing upstairs?

JUNIPER
Picking out clothes.

JUSTIN
Oh.

JUNIPER
Are you uncomfortable?

JUSTIN
Why would I be?

JUNIPER
We're all alone.

(She takes a step forward. Justin takes a step back.)

JUNIPER (Cont.)
Just you and I.

(She takes another step. He backs away some more.)

JUSTIN
Uh, yeah.

JUNIPER
Are you in love with Brandi?

JUSTIN
(Not sure how to respond.)
Uh, we went to junior prom.

JUNIPER
Do you keep a photo of her in your
wallet?

JUSTIN
Uh, my phone. (Takes out cell phone.)

JUNIPER
That's a good sign. (*Looks at picture.*)
She looks very happy.

JUSTIN
She's the most beautiful girl I know.

JUNIPER
What about Megan?

JUSTIN
(*Laughs, uncomfortable again.*)
You really are a different sort of person.

JUNIPER
Is that a nice way of saying I'm weird?

JUSTIN
I guess.

JUNIPER
So Megan isn't beautiful?

JUSTIN
Megan's a good friend of mine. I really
care about her too. But it's not the
same. She and I—

(*Megan enters.*)

MEGAN
Justin. Hi.

JUSTIN
Hey, Meg.

JUNIPER
Justin says that he cares about you—

JUSTIN
Whoa, whoa—

MEGAN
Juniper!

JUNIPER
What?

MEGAN
(To Justin.)
Can you give us a second?

JUSTIN
Sure. *(Takes cell phone, goes up stage.)*

MEGAN
(Angry whisper.)
What have you been saying to him?

JUNIPER
I've just been asking questions?

MEGAN
Did he say that he still likes me?

JUNIPER
Yes. He likes you very much.

MEGAN
But what about Brandi?

JUNIPER
He said she's beautiful.

MEGAN
So then he likes both of us. Fine. I
know what I want to wish for.

JUNIPER
Oh good.

MEGAN
I wish Justin would see Brandi as...
ugly.

JUNIPER
But Brandi's feelings---

MEGAN
Well, she hurt my feelings when she
started going out with him. Besides, it's
just temporary. It'll be enough time for
Justin to remember how much he likes
me.

JUNIPER
But it could—

MEGAN
That's my wish, Juniper. Now make it
happen.

JUNIPER
(Sad.)
Okey-doke.

(Brandi enters wearing a dress.)

BRANDI
Justin.

71

JUSTIN
(Back to her, turning.)
Hey. Happy sixth month anniversary.
(He sees her and reacts as if he has seen a warthog wearing an evening gown.)
Aaagh! Ugh! *(Jumps back in disgust.)*

BRANDI
What's wrong? *(Twirls in dress.)*
Don't you like it?

JUSTIN
It's not the dress that's the problem. I never realized that one of your nostrils is larger than the other. It's freakish. And those eyebrows of yours, and your ears – ugh!

BRANDI
(Trying to be amused.)
Ha, ha, very funny.

JUSTIN
I'm not trying to be funny. I'm dead serious. You look different. In a very, very bad way.

BRANDI
What are you talking about?!

JUSTIN
All I know is that you look—

BRANDI
What?

JUSTIN
Repulsive. I can't look at you! I think
I'm going to be sick.

GARY
You can use my fruit bowl.

JUSTIN
I have to go.

BRANDI
Justin?

*(He looks back, starts to gag, then runs off
stage.)*

BRANDI
What did you do, Megan?!

MEGAN
Nothing, I—

BRANDI
What did you say to him? Justin!

*(Brandi. runs off stage. Juniper thinks about
this for a moment. Then, she starts gasping for
air as she slowly sits down on.)*

MEGAN
Juniper, what's wrong?!

(Juniper bursts into sobs.)

JUNIPER
(In between sobs.)
Brandi... I can feel how bad she feels...
And I did that...

MEGAN
No, no, Juniper. Calm down. Listen to
me. It's not your fault. I'm the one who
made the wish.

JUNIPER
Poor Brandi… why did I do that to her?

GARY
Nice job, Megan.

MEGAN
Shut up. I didn't know.

*(Juniper is now sobbing, trying to stop but
unable to do so.)*

MEGAN
Go get a warm wash cloth or something.

*(Gary rushes off stage. Juniper is rocking back
and forth, hugging herself.)*

MEGAN
I won't do it again, Juniper. I promise.
I'll fix things with Brandi and Justin.
It was just a joke. I'll make her feel
better, just please stop crying.

(Gary returns.)

GARY
(Shows Juniper a colorful button.)
Juniper. I found this cool button. You
can have it.

*(For a few seconds Juniper cries, un-phased.
Then, she is suddenly calm, curious.)*

JUNIPER
What kind is it?

GARY
It's an antique.

JUNIPER
"Vote for Clinton."

MEGAN
(Pinning button on Juniper's jacket.)
You had us worried.

(Juniper lets out a few more sputters and a final sigh.)

JUNIPER
I don't think very far ahead and so a lot
of good ideas—ideas that sound good to
me, turn out bad or sad. Then I-I-I-I just
feel like I'm the pair of scissors that's
cut the string of a balloon. Gram told
me, she said this week, I'm on my own,
and I have choices to make, and I don't
always have to say yes to everyone. But,
I didn't want to say no to you, Megan.

MEGAN
Why not?

JUNIPER
Because I love you. Does that sound
stupid?

GARY
Kind of.

MEGAN
Shut up, Gary.

MEGAN
If it makes you feel so bad,
why didn't you just tell me no?

JUNIPER
Because I wanted to make you happy.

MEGAN
Look, I'll call Brandi and apologize.

GARY
Ha! What are you going to say?
You cast a magic spell on her
boyfriend? Face it, Megan, you single-
handedly destroyed their relationship.

MEGAN
Then tomorrow we'll make another
wish.

GARY
But I'm next!

MEGAN
Shut up; we've got to fix this first.

JUNIPER
Did you really go on a date with Justin?

MEGAN
Yes. But it was a long time ago?

JUNIPER
Was it fun?

GARY
That's when the "incident" happened.

JUNIPER
What incident?

MEGAN
Don't talk about the incident!

JUNIPER
What happened?

GARY
Justin and Megan were sitting on the
porch swing.

MEGAN
Gary! *(Throws a shoe at him.)*

GARY
Ow! And they were kissing!

(Megan throws her other shoe at him.)

JUNIPER
Did you really kiss Justin?

MEGAN
Just for a little bit. Then mom came
home early. She drove up the driveway,
flipped on her high beams, and she
could tell by the shape of his shadow
that I was with someone. So she started
honking the horn and flashing her lights.
Justin hopped off the porch and ran
across the yard, terrified. It scared him
off so bad, he didn't ask me out again.

GARY
And then Brandi swooped in.

(Megan glares at him.)

JUNIPER

I kissed a boy once. At least I tried.
I don't know if it counts if they don't
kiss back. But I tried to kiss a boy and
it almost worked. Most of the time
Gram and I don't get to see others much,
but once in a while we travel 56.8 miles
and go to town. And Gram says I just
have to be careful to mind my manners,
and don't make eye contact.
She's not the most trusting grandmother;
she does not care for strangers. The
town is nothing much to look at. Only
one video store. Two churches.
And the park only has two swings and a
pool that never gets filled up anymore.
But in that little town there is a boy
named Samuel. He's a bag-boy at the
grocery store. He does it just right and
never squishes the eggs. And he has red
hair and green eyes. And...
(Laughs at the memory.)
Freckles all over his face! And Samuel
is so nice. So nice to me and Gram. He
would always smile and always say
"thank you" and "your welcome."
If he says, "Have a nice day," then you
do. That's how good he is at his job.
And I always wanted... I always wanted
to be close to him, or to talk
to him, without Gram around. And one
day when Grandma had a really bad
cold I got to go to the store all by
myself. And I bought some oyster
crackers and some cough syrup. Then I
got to watch Samuel all by myself.
Watch him do his bag boy job.
I just stared and stared, trying to count

JUNIPER (Cont'd.)
all of those handsome freckles. Then,
he asked if there was anything else I
wanted. I just whispered "Yes."
(Pauses, closes eyes in remembrance.)
And then I grabbed him by the ears and
MmmmmmmMM!
*(Pretends she's grabbing and kissing
him.)*
That was my first kiss. My only kiss. It
was the most romantic moment of my
life. And then the manager pulled me off
of him.

(She sighs at the wonderful memory.)

(Lights out.)

SCENE FOUR
*(Lights up... It is the next morning. Mom is on
her way to work. Dad enters.)*

MOM
(Talking on cell phone.)
Tomorrow? Perfect? Wonderful. No,
it's not short notice. Everything will be
ready. Uh-huh. Okay, great, bye-bye.

DAD
So, have you made up your mind?

MOM
About what? Oh, tomorrow. I can't.

DAD
Why not?

MOM
A tea party with Ms. Dunbar.

DAD

Ugh. That old prune. Talk about a
weekend killer.

MOM

It's business, David. You should
appreciate that. You're the one who
taught me how to be a work-a-holic.

DAVID

I've been trying to change.

(Megan enters.)

MOM

And yet you're busier than ever.

DAD

I'm just trying to stay out of debt. It's
not easy paying for a mortgage and my
apartment.

MEGAN

Can I interrupt this moment of bliss?

MOM

What is it?

MEGAN

Gary is bothering Juniper. I need you
to make him stop.

*(Juniper enters, covering her ears. Gary
follows.)*

JUNIPER

La, la, la, la. I'm not listening.

GARY
Come on. Listen to me. It's my turn!
I'll split all the money with you.

MOM
Gary Matthew, stop bothering your
cousin.

GARY
But—

MOM
Look, I'm late enough as it is.

DAD
Hey, I'll drive you into town.

MOM
I have my own car.

*(She exits. The Dad looks at the kids; they look
disappointed.)*

DAD
Well, I'm trying.

GARY
Try harder, Dad.

*(Gary exits. Dad, feeling awkward, shrugs and
leaves.)*

MEGAN
(Sighs.)
Too much drama.

JUNIPER
Uncle David looked so sad.

MEGAN
Let's take care of one problem at a time.
Gary didn't waste another wish, did he?

JUNIPER
I think he wanted to, but I kept my ears
plugged.

MEGAN
You know, just because you hear
someone make a wish doesn't mean you
have to grant it. Right?

JUNIPER
Right. But it's hard. He looks so
miserable if you tell him no.

MEGAN
Well, get used to it. Okay, now, I want
things to be back to normal with Brandi
and Justin.

JUNIPER
You want—

MEGAN
I want them to be a couple again.

JUNIPER
That's so sweet, Megan.

MEGAN
What?

JUNIPER
You love Justin so much that you're
willing to let go of him.

MEGAN
Yeah, whatever, let's just fix things.

JUNIPER
But how?

MEGAN
I'll wish for it.

JUNIPER
You need to be more specific than that.

MEGAN
Okay. I wish Justin and Brandi
would... uh... hmm... how do I phrase
this? I wish that they... I wish
something would happen so they would
fall back in love.

JUNIPER
(A bit worried.)
Okie-doke.

MEGAN
You look worried.

JUNIPER
It's better to be more specific.

MEGAN
Oh, should I take it back?

JUNIPER
Too late.

*(Brandi enters. Her leg is in a cast. She walks
using crutches.)*

BRANDI
Megan!

MEGAN
Brandi! What happened to you?

BRANDI
I tripped and fell down the porch steps.
I thought I was going to die. And all I
could think about was the last thing I
said to Justin. And how much I want to
see him again.

*(Justin enters. He is walking on crutches. His
foot and ankle is all wrapped up.)*

JUSTIN
Brandi?

BRANDI
What happened to you?

JUSTIN
My brother ran over my foot with the
forklift. And while he was rushing me to
the hospital, all I could think about was
how much I hurt you yesterday… I'm so
sorry…

BRANDI
But Justin… why did you say those
things?

JUSTIN
I don't know. I was crazy. I guess I was
scared.

BRANDI
Scared?

JUSTIN
Scared to admit how much I love you.

BRANDI
Oh! I love you too!

(They hobble toward one another and embrace.)

JUSTIN
Ow.

BRANDI
Ow.

JUSTIN
Ow.

BRANDI
Ow.

(They continue to groan and snuggle as they hobble off together.)

JUNIPER
Is love always this painful?

MEGAN
It only gets worse.

GARY
I hope their relationship lasts longer
than a day.

JUNIPER
I think it will.

MEGAN
Really?

JUNIPER
Magic is temporary. Love isn't.

MEGAN
How corny.
(Thinks about this.)
Love isn't temporary.
(Sudden idea.) Gary!

GARY
(He has the same idea.)
Mom and Dad?

MEGAN
Mom and Dad. But without broken limbs.

JUNIPER
You guys aren't mad at each other, are you?

GARY
No, Juniper, I think for the first time in our life—

MEGAN
We finally agree on something.

LIGHTS OUT. END OF ACT TWO.

ACT THREE. SCENE ONE.

*(A table has been placed on stage. It has been
elegantly decorated for a pleasant tea party.
Mom is finishing the final touches. Gary enters
– he wears a tie.)*

> MOM
> There. Now you look like a handsome
> gentleman.

> GARY
> This tie is choking me.

> MOM
> It's all part of being a grown up.

(Megan and Juniper enter.)

> MOM
> Hello ladies. Oh, I have to get my
> camera.

(She dashes into the house.)

> MEGAN
> Juniper, now that we finally have a
> moment, there's something I want to tell
> you…

> JUNIPER
> You want to make another wish.

> MEGAN
> Well, it's about that. It wasn't right for
> Gary and I to fight over you.

> JUNIPER
> Because you're good friends now.

MEGAN
Well, I guess—

GARY
Not really.

JUNIPER
Because you love each other!

(She grabs both Megan and Gary and pulls them into a group hug, squeezing them hard. Mom steps out onto the porch, camera in hand.)

MOM
Say cheese!

MEGAN and JUNIPER
Cheese.

GARY
(Voice rasping.)
Personal space!

(She takes a picture.)

MOM
Wonderful. (Juniper lets go of her cousins.) Now, we only have a moment before they arrive. And remember, these women are not only friends, but potential clients. Let's make sure they have a pleasant afternoon, all right?

(A woman walks on stage, dressed appropriately for the tea party. She is older and much more prudish than Mom. It's as though you can tell just by the flicker of her eyelashes that she thinks

she's better than all those around her. She is
Mrs. Dunbar.)

DUNBAR
Ms. Pomerville.

MOM
Mrs. Dunbar. How wonderful of you to
join us.

DUNBAR
Why, Debra, what a beautiful lawn.

MOM
You've met Megan and Gary. And this
is my niece, Juniper.

(Dunbar shakes Juniper's hand. She talks
loudly and slowly.)

DUNBAR
Ah, the one you've told me about. The
homeschool child. *(Starts talking*
loudly.) Hello... Juniper...NICE TO
MEET YOU.

JUNIPER
Uh, hi.

(Two old, sour-faced ladies enter. Dunbar and
Mom welcome them..)

DUNBAR
Ah, and here they are, my wonderful
friends. The Stokley Sisters. Beth
Stokley and Bertha Stokley.

(The Stokley Sisters make their way to the table.
Their expressions are very bored, very

unimpressed with the surroundings. However,
Mom tries to be charming.)

> MOM
> Ladies. Nice to see you again.
> Shall we?

(Megan, Juniper, and Gary watch them exit. As
soon as the coast is clear they huddle up.)

> MEGAN
> Okay, Juniper, we want to get today's
> wish perfect. So we need your help.

> JUNIPER
> What can I do?

> MEGAN
> Can you help us make a wish that
> doesn't back fire?

> GARY
> Like the monkey paw.

> MEGAN
> We want it to be as simple and safe as
> possible.

> GARY
> We want our Mom and our Dad to
> be back together. And happy.

> JUNIPER
> Well… they are sad when they're apart.
> But then they're mad when they're
> together.

MEGAN

But if we can get them to feel the way
they used to… even if it's just for a day,
maybe they can start over.

JUNIPER

It might work.

MEGAN

Here's the thing… I know that Dad
wants her back. He just doesn't know
how to do it. And I know that
Mom still likes him. Her big problem is
that Dad would never spend enough
time with her.

GARY

And Dad doesn't have a clue about
that romance stuff.

MEGAN

Exactly. So she's got to see that side of
him.

GARY

So, we need Dad to become this super-
cool romantic stud who's head over
heels in love with Mom! We'll
wish for that!

JUNIPER

Okey doke.

MEGAN

(Covering up Juniper's mouth.)
Wait, wait, wait! Did we just wish for
that?

(Juniper nods slowly.)

MEGAN
Can we take it back?

(Juniper slowly shakes her head "no.")

MEGAN
(Angry.)
Gary!!!

GARY
But I didn't wish for it—I mean, I—
Agh!

MEGAN
You said the "W" word. And you only
made half of the right wish. If only
Dad's head over heels, and Mom's not
equally in love, what do you think is
going to happen?

(Mom steps out onto the porch..)

MOM
So that's our humble little home. And
now ladies, if you'd like to join me out
here…

*(Dad walks onstage. He wears his mechanic's
jumpsuit. There are greasy smudges on his
hands, sleeves, and various spots on his clothes.)*

DAD
Debbie, I want you back. You are the
light in my life and I was a fool to let
that glow fade away from me. Please
forgive me.

(Mrs. Dunbar and the Stokely Sisters watch as fascinated spectators.)

MOM
David, is this some kind of joke?.

DAD
Not at all, my love. I've been doing a lot of thinking in the last few minutes. And I've come to realize that my life is incomplete without you. We're two halves of the same whole.

MOM
I don't know what you're talking about.

DAD
I'm going to change, starting today. Instead of working late at the shop, I'm going to be here at home making you a candlelit dinner. Instead of having poker night with the boys, I'm going to have family night with the kids. *(He looks at Megan and Gary.)* Hi kids. *(Gushing.)* I love you!

MOM
But the divorce papers--

DAD
Forget we ever spoke of it. I want to marry you all over again. Debra...
(Gets down on one knee, opens up a ring box.)
Would you do me the honor.

(Ms. Dunbar and the ladies gasp.)

JUNIPER
(Jumping and clapping her hands.)
Yea! This is so romantic!

MOM
This is a piece of socket wrench.

DAVID
It's a symbol of my love for you.
I don't want to work on cars anymore.
I want to work on our marriage. And
I'm not afraid to get my hands dirty.

MOM
David... I don't know what
to say.

DAD
Don't say anything.

*(He pulls her close and kisses her. She is
surprised by this, and doesn't like it at all,
mainly because of his oily, greasy hands that are
touching her nice clean clothes. She pulls
away.)*

MOM
David! You are not going to ruin this tea
party. This is not the time or the place.

DAD
But what about us? I love you.

MOM
If you loved me you would go away and
leave me alone.

DAD
And that would prove my love for you?

                    MOM
        Yes, fine whatever, just get out of here.

                    DAD
        Then adieu, my dear one. My sweet
        heart. My angel of l—

                    MOM
        GO!!!!!

                    DAD
                (Quickly.)
        Farewell, my love!

*(He dashes off stage. Mom lets out an
exasperated sigh.)*

                    MOM
        Thank you for your patience. I'm sorry
        you had to witness that.

                    DUNBAR
        No, not at all. You might think I'm a
        Nosie-Nellie for saying this, but David
        really seems sincere, doesn't he?

                    MOM
        Oh no, not at all. He's just trying to---

*(Music drifts through the air. Romantic music.
Accordion music.)*

                    DUNBAR
        Do you hear something?

                    MOM
        I do. What is that?

MEGAN
Uh-oh.

*(Megan's Dad David enters. He is accompanied
by Phil and Bill. Phil plays the accordion, and
Bill plays some makeshift percussion
instrument—perhaps a homemade xylophone
made from spare parts.)*

*(Phil and Bill continue to play. By this time,
though, Dad is standing up on the table. Mom is
mortified. The once dignified ladies are
confused and astounded. During the musical
interlude, Dad speaks in a low voiced, Barry
White style, very smooth and sultry. He uses a
spoon for a microphone.)*

*(Optional: Depending on the director's
preference, the Dunbar brother's could forgo
their appearance here, and instead, the same
actors could be portraying the dour Stokely
Sisters. That could be pretty darn funny.)*

DAD
Debra, baby, I miss you so very much.
I miss the way you take three scoops of
ice cream, stick them in a bowl and put
it in a microwave to get it all melty and
drink it with a straw. And I miss the
way that you and I used to look at each
other, when we'd wake up from a nap.
And maybe most of all, I miss that little
wrinkle in between your eyes,
right above the ridge of your nose, that
crinkled expression you'd give me
whenever you got angry. The one
you're doing right now!

MOM
David, stop being so ridiculous and GET
OUT OF HERE! Get off of my table.

(He hops down. The music has stopped.)

DAD
Do you really want me to leave?

MOM
Yes!

DAD
I don't believe you.

MOM
Fine, then we're going inside. Ladies,
I'm sorry for all of this, why don't we—

DAD
Tango!

*(Phil and Bill play a tango. Dad grabs Mom's
hand and pulls her into a reluctant dance. As
the music plays, Dad is always moving to the
passionate rhythm of the melody. He's actually
quite graceful. In contrast, Mom isn't dancing,
she's resisting. And throughout this impromptu
"dance number," she tries to avoid him, but (as
is usually the case in a tango) he pursues.)*

*(Movement suggestions:
He grabs her hand, pulls her center stage. She
yanks her hand free. He quickly maneuvers
himself in front of her. To the rhythm of the
music he suddenly claps twice. She is very
annoyed, turns and marches in the opposite
direction. He dances around and appears
directly in front of her once more. This time, she*

slaps his face twice, keeping with the beat of the music.)

(The dance continues. She tries to shun him; he is, like Pepe Le Pew, insistent on staying together. Depending on how one choreographs the scene, she might resort to throwing paper plates or sugar in his face. They might dance around the table, perhaps up and over the table. As it progresses, he actually starts to win her over; she is actually enjoying herself!)

(By the end of the tango, she is amused by what's going on, and is dancing instead of resisting. The ladies are swooning, impressed with David's seductive ability.)

DUNBAR
Take him back, honey! If you don't I will!

(At the tango's finale, Dad has Mom in her arms. He dips her and gives her a quick kiss. She can't help but laugh. Megan, Gary and Juniper stand up and applaud.)

Lights out. End of Scene.

SCENE TWO.

(Mom and Dad sit on the porch swing (or the edge of the stage). She is snuggled beside him. They both wear blissful expressions.)

MOM
(Very content.)
Well… You realize that most separated couples go through this little phase. You know, one last fling and all that.

DAD

Don't worry. This isn't a fling.

MOM

It's just that I've never seen you like this. I mean, you're so open with your feelings.

(The lights have come up by this time to reveal a bit more of the stage. Megan, Gary and Juniper observe from a hiding spot upstage.)

GARY

I think it's working.

MEGAN

It's getting dark. What'll happen when the sun goes down?

JUNIPER

I don't know.

(An accordion softly plays.)

MOM

It's a gorgeous sunset.

DAD

The end of a wonderful day. The beginning of a beautiful evening. The twilight air is so refreshing. It's an air filled with love. How many lovers are out tonight, watching that same sky?

(Optional Moment: More lights come up to reveal Phil, Bill and the Beth and Bertha Stokley. Phil is playing the accordion. The sisters lean against each brother, gazing

wistfully into the distance. The two women look at each other approvingly.

The both give an approving: "Hmmmmm!!!"

Phil and Bill look at each other and simultaneously let out a non-committal: "Eh..."

Their lights fade, and the focus returns to Mom and Dad.)

>   DAD
>   It's so relaxing here. I don't know why
>   I'm so sleepy all of a sudden.

>   MOM
>   Well, you have been dancing all day
>   long.

(He leans his head against hers and then suddenly nods off to sleep. A moment passes and he lifts his head back up, lets out a yawn, and opens his eyes. He acts as though he's been asleep for a long time. He turns his head away from Mom.)

>   DAD
>   Oh, what a strange--

(He turns his head back and sees who he is sitting next to. His eyes open wide and he jumps to his feet.)

>   DAD
>   What the--?! Was I doing the tango?

>   MOM
>   Did you want to do it again?

(She approaches him. He's a bit scared and backs away.)

DAD
Hey, hey, hey. What's going on here?

MEGAN, GARY and JUNIPER
Uh-oh. *(They discreetly exit.)*

MOM
David?

(She takes his hand, worried.)

DAD
You're holding my hand?

MOM
Oh, I get it. You can come onto me, but I can't approach you. That is so typical.

DAD
But, but… uh, why would you be holding my hand, or be sitting with me and all that… We're not together anymore… *(Remembering.)*
But… I kissed you for some reason.

MOM
For some reason?!

DAD
Look, I don't even know what's going on here.

MOM
Then let me explain things to you.
You're trying to play with my emotions.

As usual, you're afraid of being close to me.

MOM

Really?

(She steps forward. He steps back, scared.)

MOM
See!

DAD
(Struggling.)
Now wait now, I think that we... I mean, I just feel...

MOM
What? What do you feel?

DAD
I don't know.

MOM
I know. Good night, David.

(He opens his mouth, only to find no words. He turns and leaves. She exits.)

(Lights fade.)

SCENE THREE:

(Early morning, still dark. Juniper sits by herself, downstage center. Megan enters.)

MEGAN
What are you doing up so early?

JUNIPER
A dream woke me up. They do that
sometimes. I thought she was holding
me again.

MEGAN
Grandma?

JUNIPER
No. My... my mother.

MEGAN
You see her in your dreams?

JUNIPER
It's always the same.

MEGAN
What happens?

JUNIPER
It's more like a memory. When I'm a
little kid. I'm in the old apartment.
I'm at my birthday party. There's no
kids. Just Mom. There are seven
candles on the cake and I'm wondering
why I don't have any friends. I have a
pointy hat on and I have my favorite
overalls on. And I'm sitting in front of
the cake. And after I blow the candles
out, Momma holds me and hugs me, and
I can feel her tears run down my neck.
And then she's gone. And then I wake
up.

MEGAN
Oh.

(Awkward pause.)

JUNIPER
She ran away because of me.

MEGAN
That can't be true, Juniper.

JUNIPER
I think it is.

MEGAN
Maybe she'll come back someday.

JUNIPER
Maybe.

MEGAN
Juniper… you know what? *(A moment.)*
You're a good friend.

JUNIPER
Really?

(Megan nods.)

MEGAN
One of my best. It just took me
A long time to see it.

JUNIPER
You've always been my best friend.
Even if we are family.

(Gary enters.)

GARY

Are you trying to get a jump on me
this morning?

MEGAN

No.

GARY

Good. It's my turn to make a
wish.

MEGAN

It's not anybody's turn. Except
Juniper's.

GARY

What are you talking about?

MEGAN

When I found out about Juniper's gift, I
made that big long list of all the things *I*
wanted. I mapped out a wish for
everyday that Juniper was here
with us. But now that I really think of
it, I can't think of one that's worth
while. All summer long we've been
sitting around wishing we could do
something. And now this wonderful
person with this wonderful
ability has come into our lives and
we've been wasting it. Juniper, this is
your gift. It's yours. For you.

JUNIPER

For me?

MEGAN

Yes.

JUNIPER
But how do I—

MEGAN
Think of the birthday candles in your
dream.

JUNIPER
Right now?

(Megan nods.)

JUNIPER
Hold my hand. *(Megan holds her hand.)*
You too, Gary.

GARY
Okay.

*(Each girl closes her eyes. Gary, realizing this
is a solemn moment, closes his eyes too.)*

JUNIPER
I… I wish she was back in my life.

(Sound Cue: Wind and chimes.)

*(A woman enters. She looks similar in age and
build to Megan's Mom – but different hair, and
more ragged looking clothing.)*

JUNIPER
Mommy?

MEGAN
Aunt Rosie?

ROSIE
My baby.

(Juniper and her mother embrace.)

ROSIE

Oh my June-bug. You're so big now!
So big and beautiful. But you're still the
same, aren't you? Still such a sweet
little angel. *(They hug again.)* I missed
you so much. Do you hate me for
leaving?

JUNIPER

No, Mommy, never.

ROSIE

And, oh my stars, Megan. You are so
tall and skinny! You're almost a
woman, I can't believe it.
And Gary? So handsome. And you've
finally grown into your ears. *(Turns
back to Juniper.)* I've had so many
dreams about holding you
again. I can't believe that you're
here.

JUNIPER

Will we be together now?

ROSIE

Together.

JUNIPER

You can come back home with me and
Gram.

ROSIE

I... Juniper... if only I could... But I...

MEGAN
Aunt Rose, why did you go away?

ROSIE
I had to work some things out. And it's
taken a lot longer than I planned. But I
knew Grandma would take better care of
you, better than I could…

MEGAN
What was wrong?

ROSIE
It's complicated, I guess.

MEGAN
My mom thinks you fell in love with
some guy.

ROSIE
(Bitter laughter.)
Debra. She'll believe anything.

MEGAN
Then why did you leave?

*(Rosie lets out a sigh. She gives Megan a look
as if she would be better off minding her own
business.)*

JUNIPER
(A touch of worry in her voice.)
I think I remember.

ROSIE
But it doesn't matter now, does it?
You're here. With me. Your Mommy's
here. And how in the world did I wind

ROSIE (Cont'd.)
up here? *(The answer has already dawned on her, but she acts as if this is a revelation.)* Oh, you wished for this. *(Turns to Megan and Gary)* Or *you* wished for this. You wanted to give something back to Juniper.

(Megan smiles, but Rosie is slowly becoming colder, more serious.)

ROSIE
And what else did you wish for? How many other dreams have come true? Oh, I remember how I could rationalize each day. One day for me, the next day something for little Juniper.
We had some fun times. Didn't we, kiddo? More fun in an afternoon than others have in a lifetime. Anything we could imagine, we could have... But what does a little girl want? Simple things, really. But what did I want? Nothing at first. And then everything. You must already know, Megan... The feeling of disappointment when night comes, when the wish fades away and you are forced to wait until morning. That's when you get another chance to find a new way to be happy. How many wishes did you make, Megan? How many times did you use my daughter?

(Things are getting ugly now. Megan, Juniper and Gary all realize this, but they don't know what to do or say.)

ROSIE

There's nothing to be ashamed about. I
know what it's like. Believe me. What
about you, Gary? Get anything out of
her? You don't have to feel bad.
Juniper likes making people feel good.
That's what you live for, right sweetie?

JUNIPER

Mommy, please don't.

ROSIE

It starts out happy, but it doesn't end
that way. It ends with you miserable,
almost losing your mind, and poor
Juniper... People have been
fighting over you. Your Grandma, a
long time ago, convinced me that I was
hurting you, that I should give you up,
and somehow I believed her. That's
why I left on your birthday, honey, that
was my present to you.
I left you. And now look at my life.
I spend it waiting. Waiting, I
guess, to be a better person, so I can
come back into your life. And now I'm
wondering if old Grandma simply
wanted you all to herself. And
now she's passing you off to your
cousins, and my sister; so everyone gets
a turn. I'm not going to let that happen
to you. We'll go somewhere.
Right now--- *(Pulls on Juniper's arm.)*

JUNIPER
(Near despair.)
Mommy, please... Please Mommy,
please.

ROSIE

We'll hide until tomorrow, and then
we'll wish. We'll go anywhere we want,
anywhere we can be safe and alone and
happy.

*(Juniper pulls away. Rosie roughly grabs her
again and pulls her toward the exit.
Juniper stands her ground.)*

JUNIPER

NO!

MEGAN

Let her go!

ROSIE

She isn't yours! Juniper belongs to me!
She is *my* daughter.

JUNIPER

No. I'm not anymore. I will love you.
And I forgive you. But I don't belong to
you. I'm not yours. I'm mine. I am
mine. Let go of me.

ROSIE
(She lets go.)
Juniper. I'm so sorry. I thought I could
see you without… without becoming…

JUNIPER

I understand.

ROSIE

I used you for so long. I thought
I could be strong enough.

JUNIPER
Maybe I'm stronger now… for both of us.

(Juniper's Grandmother has entered.)

GRAM
You certainly are, my child.

(Juniper embraces her grandmother. Then Gram approaches her daughter.)

GRAM
Come, Rose. Today was the first difficult step of many.

ROSIE
Will you let me see her again?

GRAM
Yes.

ROSIE
When?

GRAM
Sometime soon. I will return in a week, Juniper. Grammy and Rose need to take care of a few matters.

ROSIE
(Being led away by Gram.)
Goodbye, Junebug.

JUNIPER
Goodbye.

(After Gram and Rosie leave, there is a moment where the others just watch off stage. Gary is upstage, away from the girls. Megan and Juniper look at each other – and they should connect. Maybe it's just with eye contact. Maybe they hold each other's hands. Or maybe it's a simple hug – but they connect, and their friendship is solidified.)

(Lights fade.)

SCENE FOUR.

(Mom comes jogging along. She's miserable, as she usually is while jogging.)

(Dad crosses in front of her, jogging as well. He's wearing some seriously ugly jogging clothes.)

MOM
David?

DAD
Good morning.

MOM
What are you doing?

DAD
I'm jogging.

MOM
You don't jog.

DAD
I just started.

MOM
Why?

DAD
Because I'm trying to improve myself.
Why do you do this?

MOM
Same reason.

DAD
How's it working so far?

MOM
I don't know yet.

DAD
Oh. Guess it takes time to see results.

MOM
I guess. How do you like it so far?

DAD
I hate it!

MOM
So do I!

(They stop jogging, out of breath and exhausted.)

DAD
But maybe we should keep it up?

MOM
I'll be on this stretch of road tomorrow.

DAD
I'll be here.

MOM
Okay. Hey, I'll race you back to the house.

DAD
Really?

MOM
Yeah. I want the kids to see you in that outfit.

(They run off.)

SCENE FIVE.

(Juniper is finishing a painting as she looks off into the distance, studying her subject. It's a painting of a tree house. Gary carries a hammer and some lumber across the stage. Megan carries a paint can.)

(Brandi and Justin enter.)

BRANDI
Oh my gosh, that is the coolest tree house ever.

JUSTIN
Did you guys build that?

GARY
Yeah. I think I have like a million splinters.

MEGAN
Boo-hoo. I almost cut off my thumb.

JUNIPER
I know, it was so fun.

BRANDI
Guess what. Today is our six and a half
month anniversary.

MEGAN
Congratulations.

BRANDI
I think since we survived the "incident,"
we'll be able to survive anything.

GARY
Good, you can test out the tree house for
us.

JUSTIN
Cool.

*(Mom and Dad jog past them. They are
laughing about something. Mom is ahead in the
race.)*

DAD
I let you win!

(They exit.)

BRANDI
Are your parents back together?

MEGAN
They aren't back together. But they're
not not together.

JUSTIN
Come on, let's go check it out.

(Justin and Brandi exit. Gram enters.)

GRAM
The van's packed and ready. Time to say our goodbyes.

MEGAN
But her painting's not finished.

JUNIPER
Keep it. I'll finish it when I come back.

GRAM
(To Megan.)
I trust you and your cousin had a nice visit.

MEGAN
Well, we wasted the first half wishing the days away. But the last week has been… just like it used to be.

JUNIPER
Maybe better.

(The grand daughters hug Gram. Gary hugs her afterwards.)

GARY
Grandma… Can I have some money?

(Mom and Dad enter the stage.)

MOM
Goodbye, Juniper. I'm going to miss you.

DAD
I'll help you back out, Renee.

GRAM
Thank you, young man. Good to see
you again.

DAD
Yeah. You too.

(They exit.)

GARY
Bye Juniper. Thanks for everything.
(She hugs him tightly. Lets go.)
Even violating my personal space.

MOM
*(Wanting Megan and Juniper to have
their moment.)*
Come on, kiddo. *(Leads Gary off stage.)*

MEGAN
Well... see you soon.

JUNIPER
Yeah. One more hug?

(They hug.)

MEGAN
Well, you better go before I burst into
tears.

JUNIPER
Bye, bye.

MEGAN
Bye.

*(Juniper leaves. As she leaves the stage Megan
starts to speak quietly.)*

MEGAN
(Sigh.) I wish we could do it all over
again.

JUNIPER (Off stage.)
Okey-doke.

(Juniper rushes onto the stage.)

JUNIPER
Megan! Megan, Megan! It's July the
Eighth, Megan. It's Friday again! Can
you believe it? Friday, July the Eighth -
- again! Isn't it wonderful?

(The girls laugh. Lights out.)

The End.

Wade Bradford is the author of over twenty plays including:

CSI: Neverland

Sleeping Beauty and the Beast

A Midsummer Night's Dream: The Musical

Conflict

Sahara Nights

JT and the Pirates

and

Romeo Revised

Visit his websites:

www.wadebradford.com

and

www.plays.about.com

Made in the USA
Lexington, KY
14 August 2011